The Angry King

1 Samuel 18—2 Samuel 5 FOR CHILDREN

Written by Yvonne Holloway McCall
Illustrated by Jim Roberts

ARCH Books
Copyright © 1976 CONCORDIA PUBLISHING HOUSE, ST. LOUIS, MISSOURI
MANUFACTURED IN THE UNITED STATES OF AMERICA
ALL RIGHTS RESERVED
ISBN 0-570-06110-5

Goliath, the wicked giant, was dead,
But Saul, the king, was filled with dread.

For people were singing
And dancing with joy.
They all loved David, the shepherd boy.

They sang, "O, Saul, you're a powerful king,
But stronger by far
Is the boy with the sling."

Saul was angry. He burned with hate.
He thought, "I'll get even
With David. Just wait.

I can tell by the way all the people sing
That next they'll want him
To be their king.
For God helps David and always will."
And this made Saul even angrier still.

And so at the palace next day after noon,
While David tried calming him
Down with a tune,
Saul, in a rage, grabbed ahold of a spear

And flung it at David;
His purpose was clear.

But David ducked quickly;
The spear struck the wall,
And he fled through the night
From the clutches of Saul.

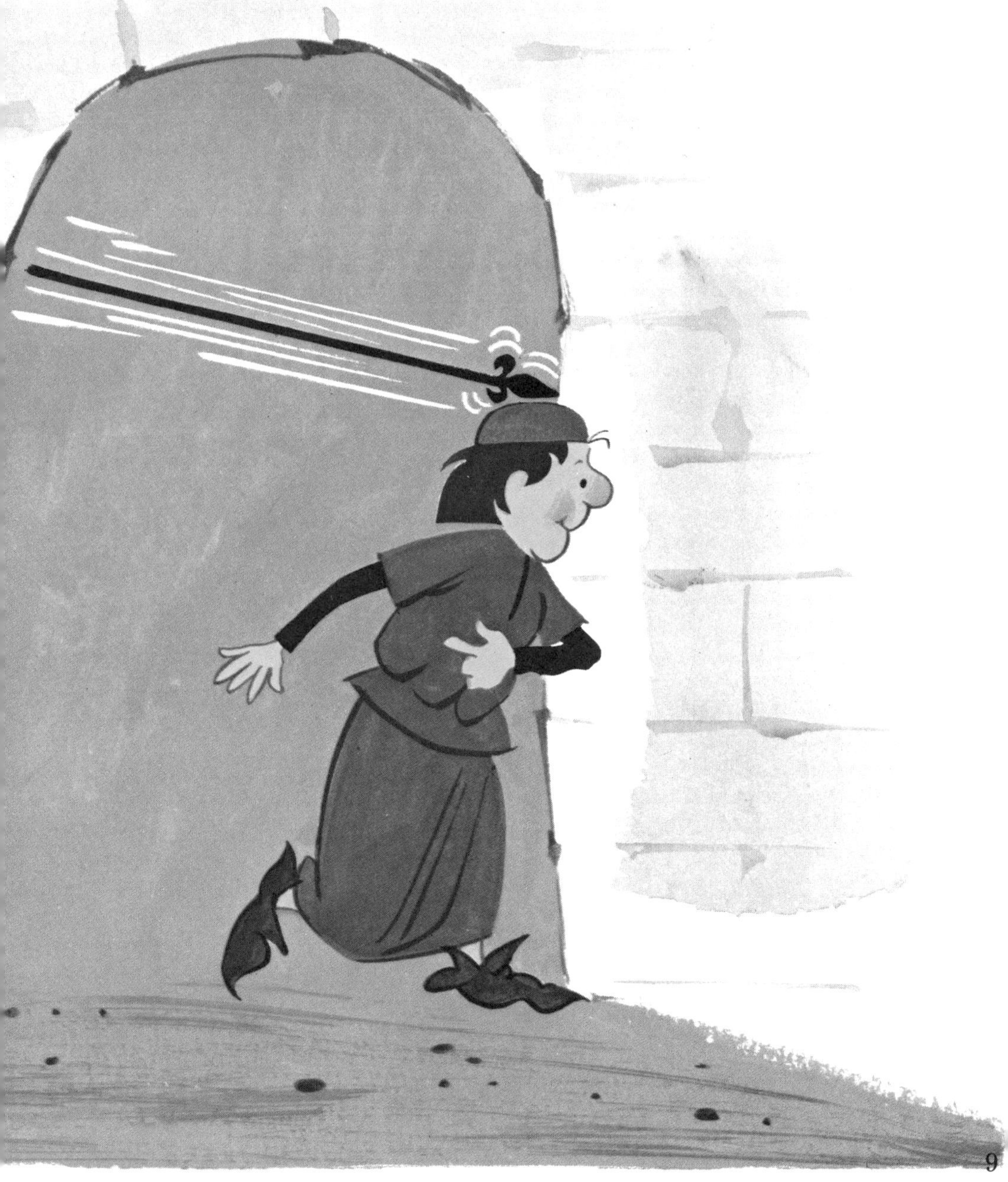

It happened again,
So with help from his wife,
David escaped and ran for his life.

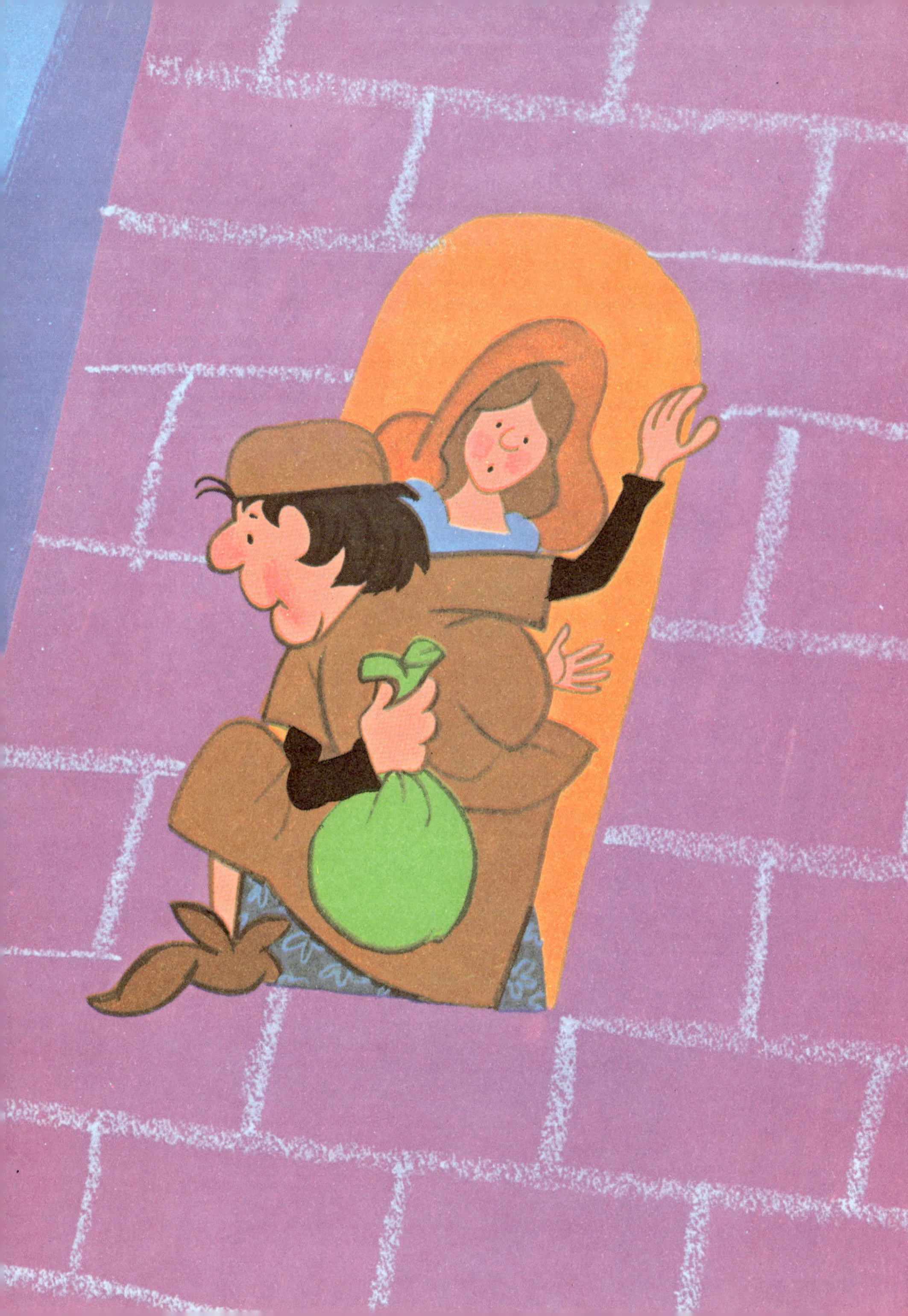

In the hills and the forests,
He hid as he fled;

A cave was his home;
The ground was his bed.
Then all of his family,
Including his brothers,
Joined with him there
With a few hundred others.

So Saul called all of his army to war,
And they hunted for David as never before—
Day after day, to the left and the right,
But God kept him hidden
And out of their sight.

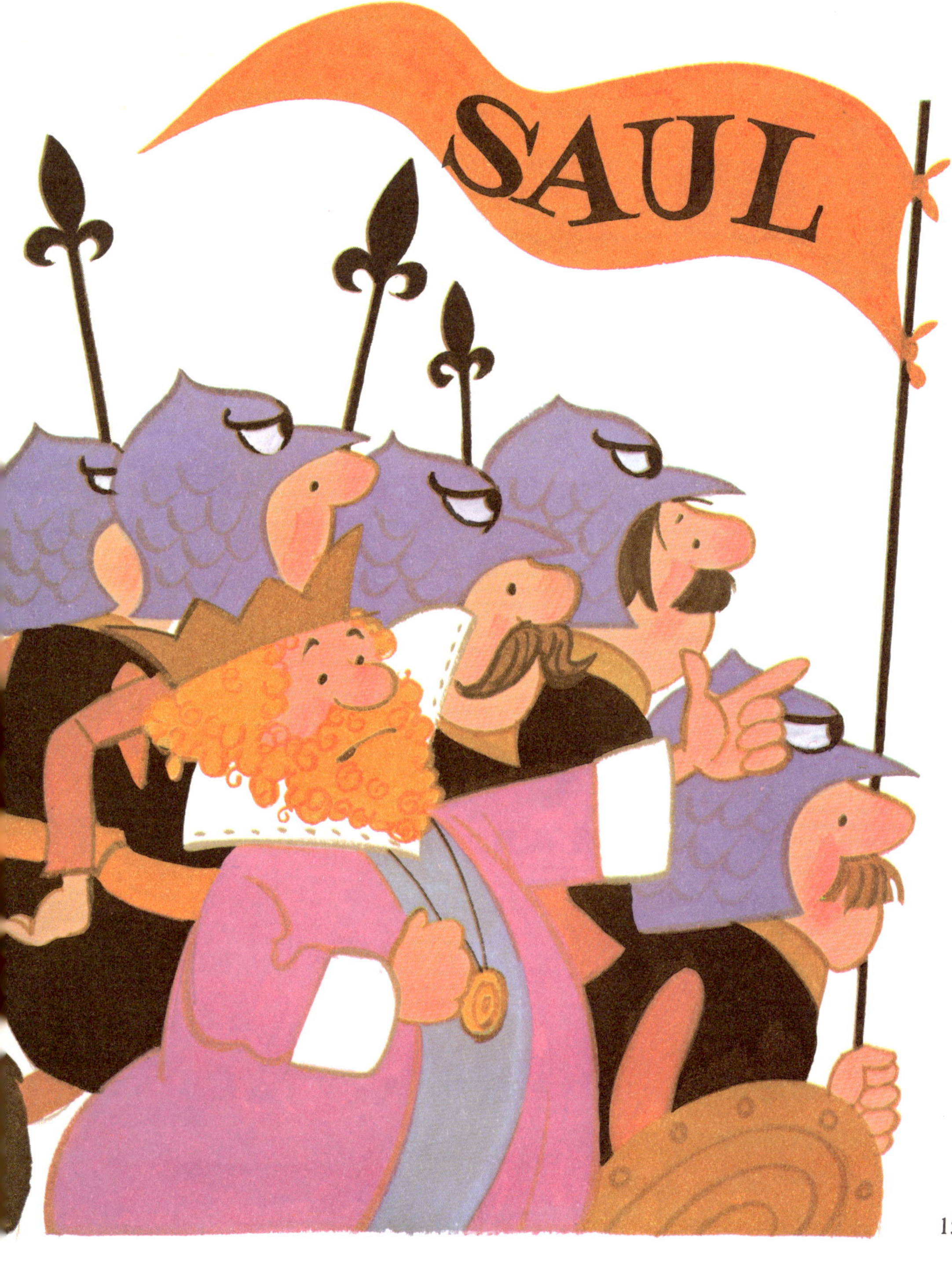
SAUL

And then in the desert, dry and stark,
Saul found a shelter—
A cave that was dark.
So into the cave Saul went striding,
Not knowing that that was
Where David was hiding.

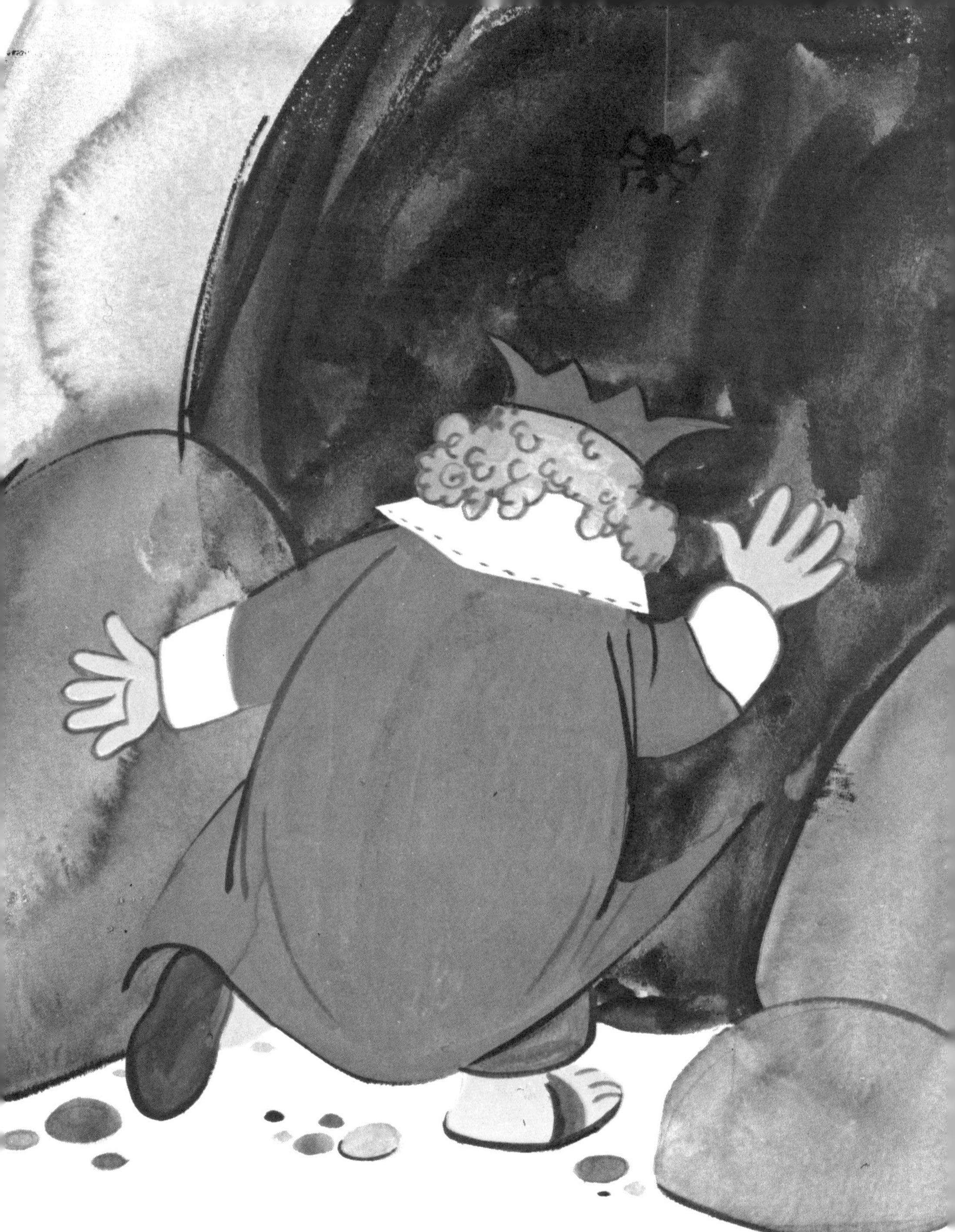

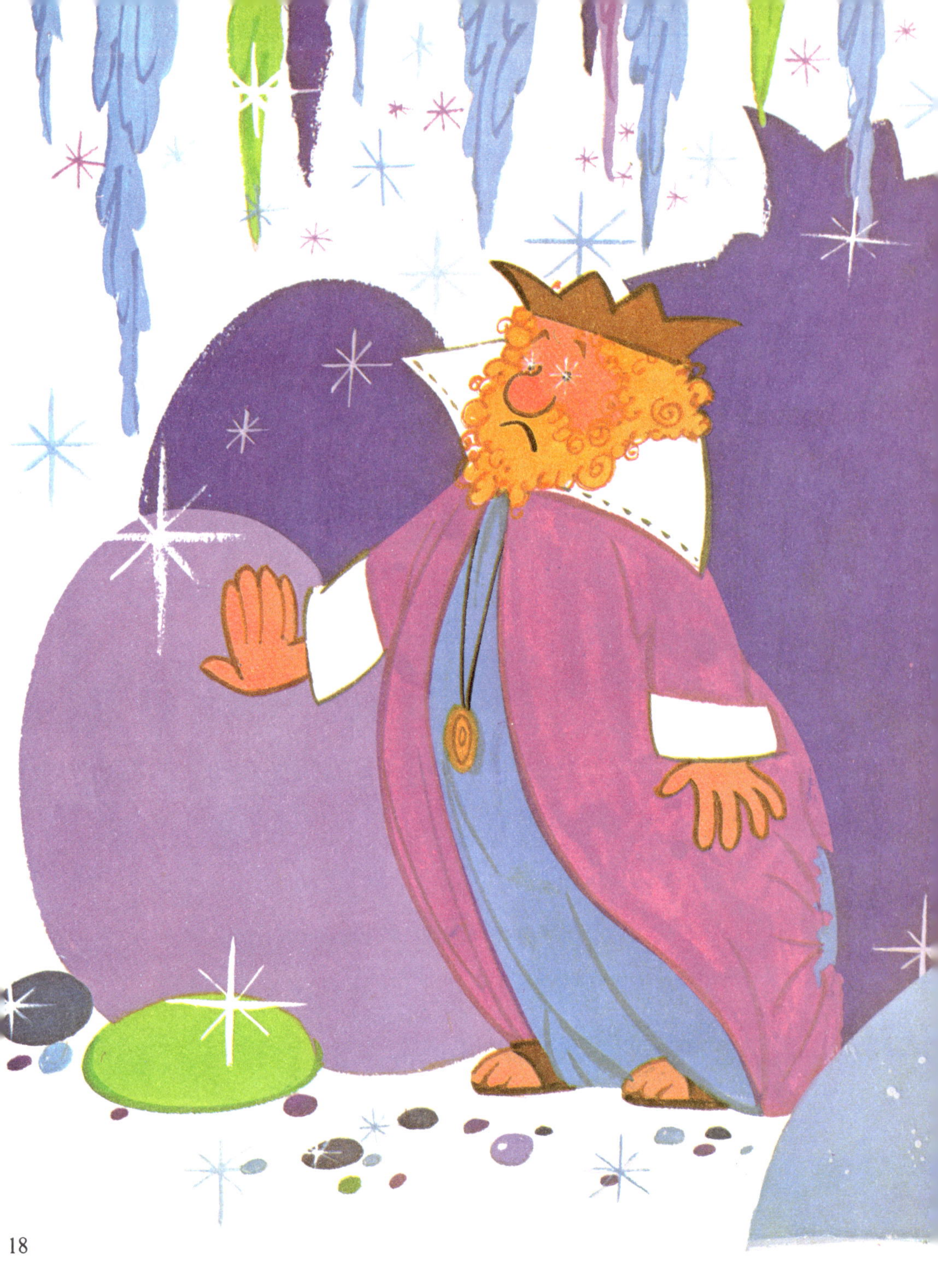

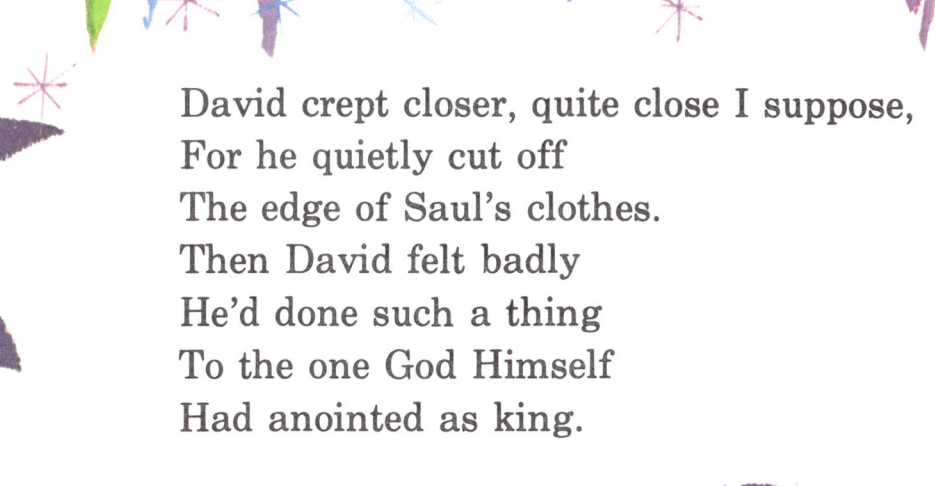

David crept closer, quite close I suppose,
For he quietly cut off
The edge of Saul's clothes.
Then David felt badly
He'd done such a thing
To the one God Himself
Had anointed as king.

So David called, "Saul";
Saul wheeled around.
And David bowed low
With his face to the ground.

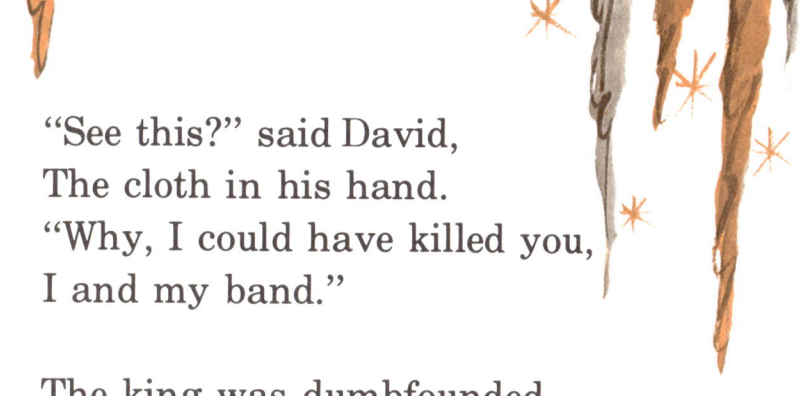

"See this?" said David,
The cloth in his hand.
"Why, I could have killed you,
I and my band."

The king was dumbfounded
And started to cry,
"Now I know for a fact
You're far better than I.

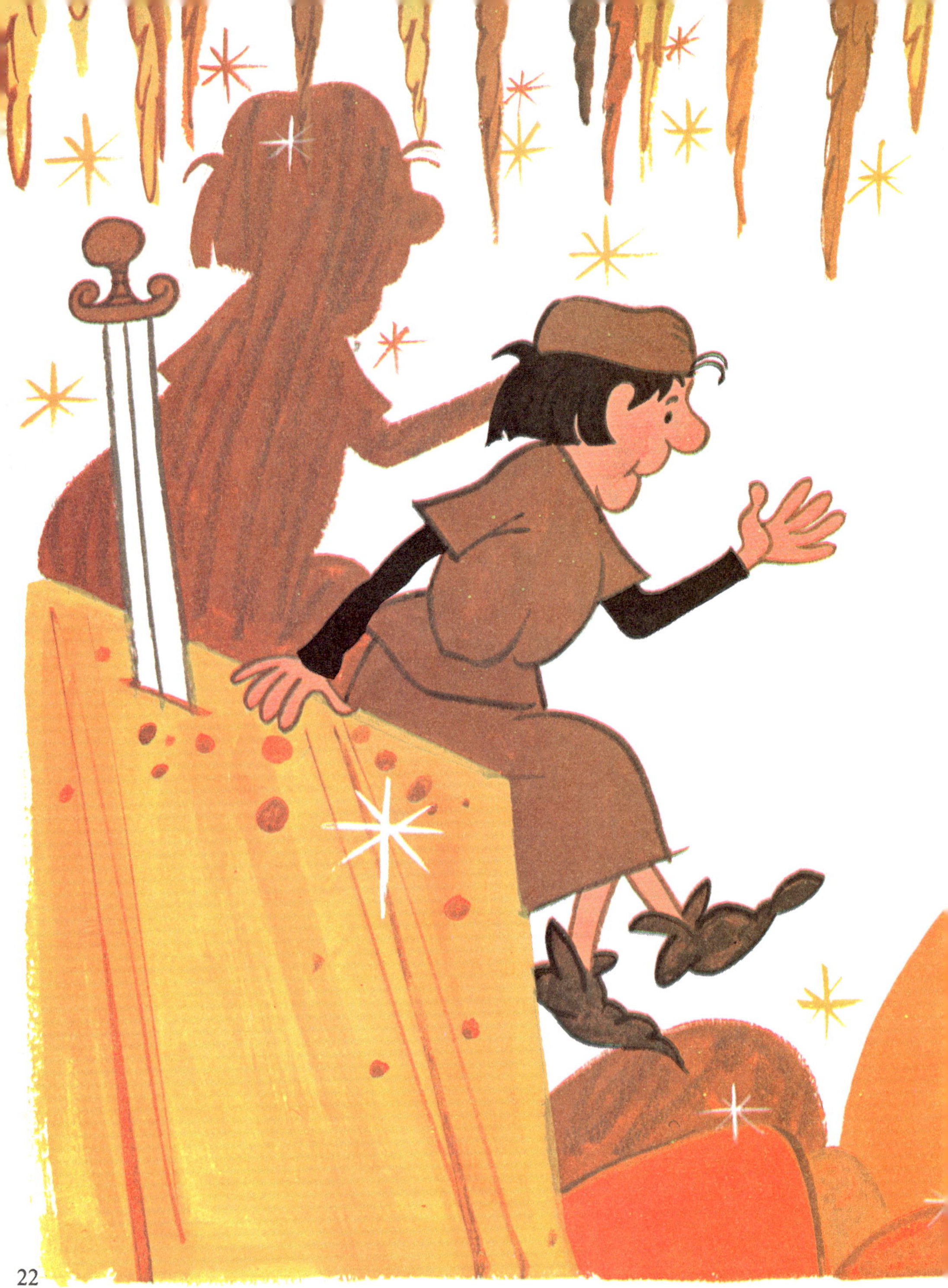

I hunted you, wanted you dead, but I find
That *I* have been evil
And you have been kind.
For who, if he stood by his enemy, armed,
Would let him go safely away, unharmed?"

Saul was ashamed and went home, but then
He started to hunt him all over again.

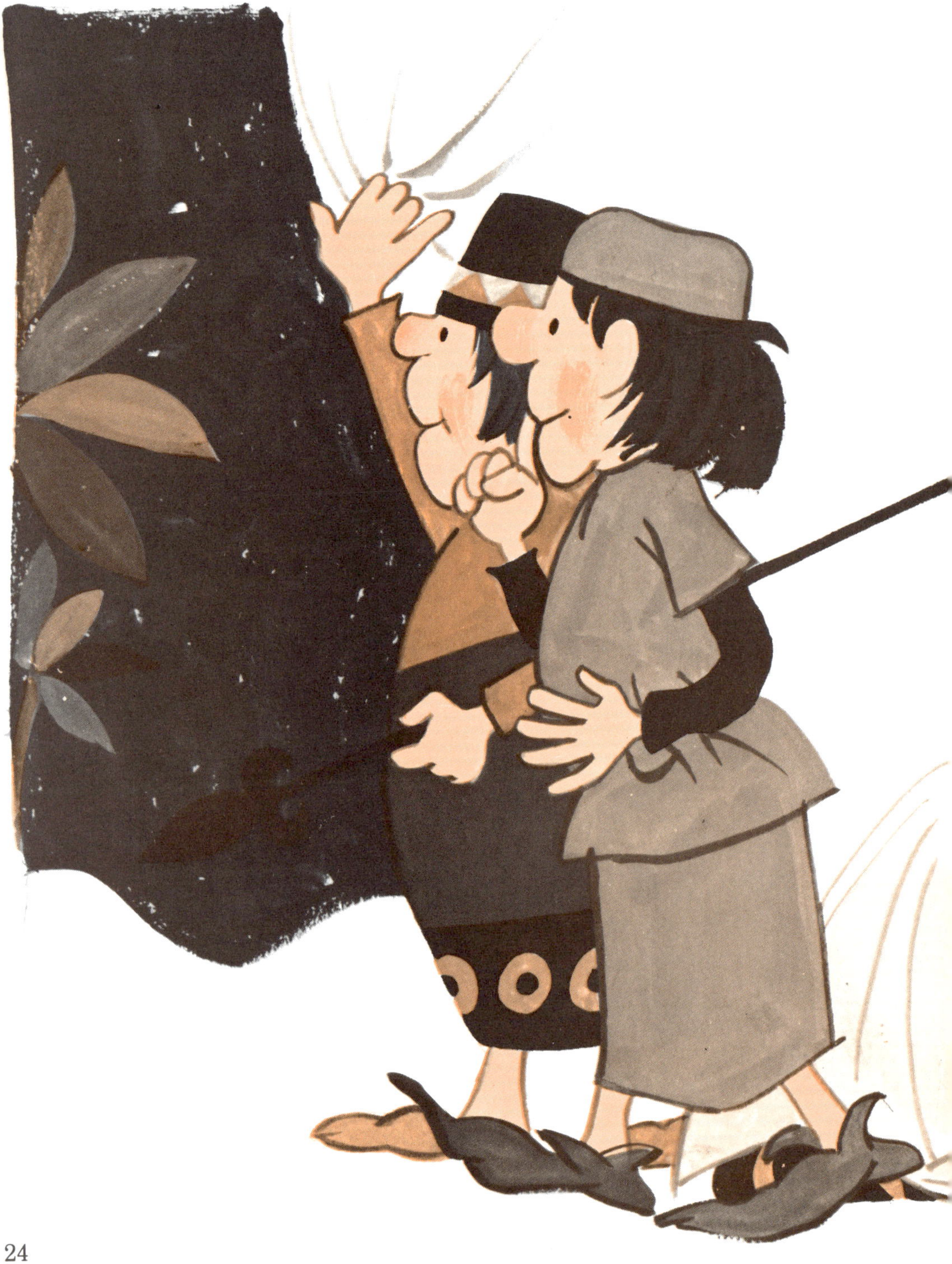

One night David and friend went creeping
Into the camp where Saul lay sleeping.
They grabbed Saul's spear
That was stuck in the ground
And tiptoed away without making a sound.
No enemy woke; each lay in a heap,
For God had put all of them
Soundly to sleep.

A safe distance off,
David turned back to call,
"Once again, I could have
Injured you, Saul.
But I didn't and won't,

Though you cause me to roam
And drove me away from my family and home.
The Lord will deliver me out of your hand
And protect me from all of
The evil you've planned."

A long time later, a battle arose,
And Saul was attacked
By his Philistine foes.

A ragged man with dust on his head
Escaped and came running to David and said,
"Saul has been killed!" And David cried
For Saul and all of the others who died.

For David was kind
And the news made him sad.
And the people were pleased
With the kindness he had.

And later they crowned him
The king over all.
And they loved him—their king,
Who was kinder than Saul.

So that's how God
Took the boy with the sling,
The shepherd, David, and made him a king.

DEAR PARENTS:

There are many lessons to be learned from this story. First, David's treatment of Saul is a perfect illustration of the love described in 1 Corinthians 13. Apply the following paragraph, sentence by sentence, to the story.

"Love is patient. Love is kind. Love isn't jealous. It doesn't brag or get conceited. It isn't indecent. It isn't selfish. It doesn't get angry. It doesn't plan to hurt anyone. It doesn't delight in evil, but is happy with the truth. It bears everything, believes everything, hopes for everything, endures everything."

It is difficult for adults and children alike to accept the fact that God loves their friends, enemies, and competitors as much as He loves them. God blesses their opponents' families and watches over their homes. David realized God loved Saul; so David treated Saul accordingly.

Second, the story illustrates real trust in God. Saul feels he must thwart God's plans if he is to remain king. David always trusts that God's way is best.

Third, the story is about competition—handling it in a godless way as Saul does or in a Christian way as David does.

Illustrate some of the above ideas with details from the story. And try to illustrate Christian morality to your children daily in your lives.

THE EDITOR